The Great Adventure of Lav Kush

Retold by: **Neelima Sinha**
Illustrated by: **Ajay Kumar**

PANDA
An imprint of Unicorn Books

The Great Adventure of Lav Kush

The Ramayana tells the story of the battle between Prince Rama and Ravana, King of Lanka. Ravana had kidnapped Sita, Rama's beautiful wife, and kept her a prisoner in his palace. Rama rescued her after a fierce battle and brought her home to Ayodhya.

Amidst great rejoicing, Rama and Sita were crowned the King and Queen of Ayodhya. Rama loved his people and did everything he could to keep them happy. But some people were not satisfied.

One day the court messenger whispered in the King's ears. "Your Majesty, please forgive me, but this is what I heard a citizen say last night to his wife, before he turned her out of the house." The man brought his lips closer. "'I would never take my wife back if she stayed away from home for so long. How could Rama do so?' I heard the man say. I heard this with my own ears, Your Majesty!" the messenger said, his face pale with fear.

Rama was shocked. 'I know Sita. She is a good wife and a gentle, noble person,' he thought. Then he shook his head. 'No, I must not be selfish. The King and Queen must be above suspicion. I must do my duty, however painful it may be for me. If people do not trust the Queen she will have to go.'

The King called his brother, loyal Prince Laxman. "Dear brother, promise me you will do as I say," he said.

"Your wish is my command, O respected one," answered Laxman, bowing low.

"Then you must take Sita to the forest and leave her there," said Rama softly.

"What? No, no, I cannot do this!" protested Laxman. But he had to obey his brother. So, he invited Sita to visit the forest. Their chariot crossed the river Ganga and entered the deep woods. Though he felt miserable, Laxman knew he had to do as ordered.

"O Lord, you are kind and merciful. Please protect the gentle Sita," he begged the gods. Then he quickly turned away to hide his moist eyes and drove off to Ayodhya.

Sage Valmiki found the weeping Queen huddled under a tree. He comforted her and offered her food and shelter. He led the grateful Queen to his home in the forest. Sita began her new life in the ashram hut. She busied herself by caring for the plants and animals and tried to forget her sorrow.

A few months later, twin sons were born to Sita. Sage Valmiki named the babies Lav and Kush. As they grew older, he taught them the Vedas and the martial arts. Their mother watched proudly as the boys developed into skilled warriors. But when they asked her about their father she simply smiled sadly. She did not reveal the secret that their father was the great King Rama of Ayodhya.

★★★★★

Years passed. Rama's kingdom flourished and his fame spread far and wide. So, the King decided to perform the Ashvamedha Yagya. If successful, it would establish him as the greatest king of all. Laxman chose a horse for the Yagya. A saddle, studded with gems, was laid on the graceful black steed. A blue peacock feather was stuck between his white ears.

"This horse belongs to great and noble King Rama of Ayodhya, whom even the gods fear. Whoever thinks he is as powerful as him may capture the horse. Others must acknowledge defeat and pay tax. Or else, flee into the forest!" proclaimed the message fixed on the horse's forehead.

Prayers were chanted and drums beaten as the graceful animal galloped away. Flowers rained down on the procession. Sixty thousand and ten of the bravest soldiers in the kingdom, led by Rama's brother, Shatrughan, followed the horse wherever it went. They defeated powerful giants who came in the way. No king dared to capture the proud steed; it trotted on, unchallenged, conquering kingdoms.

The horse then reached the forest where sage Valmiki dwelt. Lav and Kush were delighted to see the beautiful horse grazing under some trees. "O, look, brother, what a graceful creature! Let us catch him!" shouted Lav. The two went close and read the proclamation attached to the animal's forehead.

"Look what it says," laughed Kush. "Even the gods fear the King of Ayodhya! But we are not afraid. Are we?"

"Let others fear the King and flee. We are not any less brave than the most powerful," agreed his brother. The two boys caught the horse's reins and pulled him forward. They tied him to a tree and crouched near, bows drawn, ready for battle.

Soon, the general leading the army galloped into sight. As his eyes fell upon the scene, he stopped short, surprised. “What have you done? Untie the horse at once! Don’t you know whom it belongs to? The great King Rama!” he shouted.

“It may belong to anyone, but now it is ours,” grinned Lav, stroking the horse’s back.

“You do not know what you are doing, boys... Return the horse at once! Or you will have to battle a powerful army,” the general warned.

“Do not try to teach us. We know what it means to catch the horse. We are ready to fight. Are you?” taunted Kush.

“Go home, children. I allow you to do so!” ordered the general.

“Oh, so you beg us to return him? Brother, you are a disgrace as a warrior. What kind of soldier are you?” Lav said scornfully.

The general turned red, but kept calm. “Your parents will surely be proud of you. But it’s not a child’s game. Run off!”

“Great warrior, you are too weak to defend a horse with such a message! Did you think there was no one brave enough to fight you?” Kush taunted the general.

The insult made the man tremble with fury. He rushed at the two boys, his army at his heels. The twins were waiting for this. Quick as lightning they released a shower of arrows. Several soldiers hit the ground. Others turned tail and fled to the spot where Shatrughan waited. "A hermit's children have caught our horse and slain our men!" they cried.

Shatrughan could not believe it. "Children? What do you mean? Are you afraid of boys?" he scolded the soldiers. The panic-stricken men insisted he must see things for himself. Shatrughan was as surprised as the general was when he saw the boys. "My dear kids, you have obviously made a mistake. But I shall forgive you, if you hand back the animal. And I shall reward you well," he said, smiling at the young warriors.

"O Prince, why has your King sent the horse with the message then? If he is not really as powerful as he pretends to be, forget the horse. Return to the safety of the palace

walls!" their defiant reply wiped the smile off Shatrughan's face.

"How dare you challenge me? Alright, pick up your weapons and prepare to sacrifice your lives!" cried Shatrughan angrily.

"You think you can scare away lions with just a clap of your hands? Watch, then!" laughed the boys. They bowed in the direction of their guru Valmiki's hermitage and sent forth a swift shower of arrows.

The sharp shafts shattered Shatrughan's chariot into pieces. His charioteer slumped to the ground. The battlefield was soon littered with bodies of fallen warriors.

The surviving men fled back to the palace and straight to Rama's court. "Save us, save us, O King Rama!" they pleaded, shaking with fear. "The two sons of a forest hermit have felled our men! Prince Shatrughan lies injured."

Rama could not believe it. How could two youths cause such destruction to his mighty army? And then, how could his men raise weapons against the sons of a sage? He shook his head sternly, "A king's duty is to protect, not harm, learned men. Laxman, find out what is happening. And if there are some kids indulging in mischief, catch them and bring them here! But be careful, do not hurt the hermit's children," he ordered.

Laxman bowed before the King. Then he galloped to the forest at the head of his vast army. A bitter battle raged there. Two boys, golden faces blazing like two suns in the sky, sent out shafts of rays that were burning arrows. "Stop! Stop it!" Laxman commanded the warriors on the battlefield. "A King cannot fight hermits."

Then he turned to the boys, "Put your weapons down! Stop fighting... do you wish to fall victim to my fury?"

"First take a look at your noble brother!" jeered Lav, pointing at Shatrughan.

"The mighty warrior lies there, face in the dust!" cried Kush triumphantly.

"I still refuse to lift my bow against hermits. Fetch your companions!" ordered Laxman.

"We have none. Two are enough to defeat your weak and cowardly army!" said Lav scornfully.

Furious, Laxman bit his lips to control his anger. "Beware, my fury has no place for mercy. I warn you once again! Put those weapons down before misery befalls your parents!"

Kush sent a swift shower of arrows in reply. They hid the sun and darkened the sky. Laxman was forced to pick up his bow. Angrily, he drove his chariot right to the centre of the battlefield and returned the attack. Sparks flew as arrows clashed mid air. Finally Laxman swung a heavy club at Kush and threw him to the ground.

Lav lunged at Laxman. The earth shook as the two wrestled. Soon Lav crashed to the ground. But Kush was up again by now. He aimed an arrow at Laxman, who answered with a fierce volley. At last Kush picked up a special arrow called Mohan. He had learnt its use from sage Valmiki. As it hit Laxman, he fell down unconscious.

This was too much for the frightened soldiers. They fled helter-skelter back to the palace. "O King, Laxman lies defeated. The whole army is destroyed. The boys are truly valiant, though young. And they are handsome like you!" said the soldiers.

Rama's third brother Bharat bowed before the King. "Maybe the gods are punishing us for abandoning Sita," he said.

"Where is your courage?" answered Rama. "Go to the battlefield at once. Take all the horses, elephants, and chariots you require. Ask our faithful and powerful

allies to help. Get Hanuman, the mightiest of them all. Request the Monkey King Sugriva as well as Jambavan, Vibhishana, and the others to join us. Go, fetch the boys here."

It was Bharat's turn to lead the attack. Once more the army, now including the powerful monkeys and bears, marched to the battlefield. "O charming brothers, how lucky your parents are! They have such valiant sons. Go back to them," Hanuman warned the boys as soon as he saw them.

"Powerless ones, it is you who should go back. We do not fight cowards," retorted Lav and Kush.

"Ready your weapons then!" challenged Bharat.

The bears and monkeys uprooted huge rocks and trees and flung them at the boys. Lav's arrows reduced them to fragments. Chariots were shattered and heroes felled. Everywhere there was chaos and destruction. The bravery and skill of the twins created havoc as they moved swiftly, spreading fear in the enemy camp.

Bharat sent forth his bravest warriors. Heads bowed in defeat, Jambavan, Angad, Sugriva, and Vibhishana all returned. At last the twins came face to face with Bharat. His arrow struck Lav down. Then Kush, furious, drew his bowstring and shot a hundred arrows that felled the mighty warrior, Bharat. Panic stricken, the soldiers once again rushed to tell the King.

Rama decided to abandon the Yagya and see the heroes with his own eyes. On reaching close, he put his weapons down and asked the twins to come near. "You are very brave, boys. You defeated a powerful army. Tell me, who are your parents? Which village and which country do you belong to?" he asked.

"Don't talk sweetly. Why must you know who we are? Take up your weapons, unless you too are a coward in battle," challenged the twins.

"I will not fight. Not until I know who you are," insisted Rama.

"The weak tell tales when afraid to face warriors!" mocked Lav.

"Lift your bow! Are you a coward that you make excuses?" asked Kush.

Rama folded his arms and said firmly, "Before picking up

weapons one must know who the enemy is. I will not strike until I have this information."

"Our mother's name is Sita, daughter of Janak. We don't know who our father is. Sage Valmiki brought us up and named us Lav and Kush," said the boys impatiently, eager to begin the battle.

Rama listened in stunned silence. A wave of pride swept over him, but he decided to keep quiet. "Alright, let the battle begin. I shall send my warriors to fight you," he said, and put his bow aside. He did not wish to lift arms against his own sons.

The fight began once again. Rama's presence encouraged the monkeys, bears and soldiers, led by Angad, Hanuman, Sugriva and other warriors, to return to the attack with greater vigour.

It was no use. The great army rolled in the mud. Before long Hanuman and Jambavan were bound hand and foot by Lav and Kush. The boys stripped them off their jewels and weapons. Loading everything on the horse's back, they walked to their hermitage. They bowed before sage Valmiki and laid the booty at their mother's feet.

Sita recognised the jewels and weapons at once. After all, they belonged to people she knew and respected. She and sage Valmiki immediately understood everything. "Release them immediately. What have you done? You have hurt your own family and friends," cried Sita in dismay.

Valmiki patted the boys' heads approvingly. He consoled Sita and led the boys back to the battlefield where Rama was tending to the fallen and the wounded. "Behold, your sons stand humbly before you. I am proud of their skill and bravery on the battlefield," said Valmiki. He went on to relate the

story of Sita's life in the forest and the birth of the twins.

Rama gazed lovingly at the boys. Tears of pride welled up in his eyes. He drew the two closer in a warm embrace. Then he sent Laxman to fetch Sita with all honour.

The Queen arrived, looking tearful but calm. She shook her head when Rama moved towards her. Instead, she folded her hands and pleaded, "O Mother Earth, my duty is done. Please take me back into your lap."

There was a thundering sound. The earth then opened up and a beautiful throne appeared from its folds. Sita walked up to it and sat on the golden throne. The earth rumbled again as the throne began to sink back into the earth, taking Sita along.

"No, Sitey!" shouted Rama. But the throne continued to descend as the earth closed over it. Rama watched, shocked, as his beloved Sita disappeared from sight. At last he turned to his sons, Lav and Kush, "Your mother will always be pure and noble." Putting his arms around them, he said, "Come with me, my sons. Our people await us."

King Rama and the two princes returned to their palace, followed by all the others.

PANDA

Quality reading for children...

Indian Tales & Global Tales, New Tales & Folk Tales, Fables, Legends & Mythology and books on growing up well, first told or retold by children's authors

VOLUME 1-2

VOLUME 1-2

VOLUME 1-5

All books available in Hindi also

VOLUME 1-3

Guldasta

Engrossing tales for the young

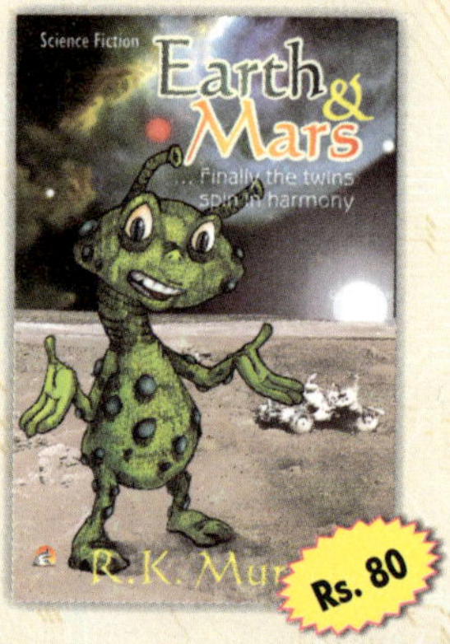

Guldasta is a collection of stories for children 10 years and older. Adventure, murder, mystery, myths, humour, horror, ghosts, science fiction and more...

Selected for AWIC's Book Review Competition for Children

Guldasta covers it all.

Guldasta – An imprint of Unicorn Books, Delhi